Happy Day 2016
Mother's Day
from Jakie
& Mal
we highly recommend
this book!

WHY IS MY DOG DOING THAT?

WHY IS MY DOG DOING THAT?

Gwen Bailey

DEALING WITH DOGGIE DON'TS

THUNDER BAY
P·R·E·S·S
San Diego, California

Thunder Bay Press
An imprint of the Baker & Taylor Publishing Group
10350 Barnes Canyon Road, San Diego, CA 92121
www.thunderbaybooks.com

ISBN-13: 978-1-60710-031-7
ISBN-10: 1-60710-031-2

Library of Congress Cataloging-in-Publication Data available upon request

Printed in China

2 3 4 5 13 12 11 10 09

Contents

Introduction

Dogs fit into our homes and lives so well that it is tempting to think of them as small, nonspeaking humans in furry skins. Although dogs do indeed share many of our emotions and behaviors, they are, of course, members of a completely different species whose ancestors lived in the wild by hunting large prey in packs. As a result, dogs may sometimes behave in ways that we find strange, embarrassing, or downright inexplicable.

This book explains why dogs do what they do. It gives reasons for some of their more curious behaviors that confuse and amaze the humans who live with them.

Dogs have a wide repertoire of behaviors that were designed to help them to learn hunting skills and survive in the wild. Although many of these behaviors are no longer needed by pet dogs—since we provide for all their needs—the desire to continue these behaviors has been passed down from generation to generation. Many of these instincts may seem strange to their human companions, but they once gave our dog's ancestors the ability to find enough food,

Sniffing in places that may seem distasteful to humans can provide dogs with lots of useful information.

to live in social groups, to defend territories, and to reproduce in the wild. So strong are these instincts that many pet dogs of today would still be able to fend for themselves without the aid of humans should they need to.

Even if you lived with dogs as a child, it is not until you own a dog yourself that you begin to look more closely at his behavior. Dogs are not so different to people in many ways, but they often do things that we would not, or could not, do. For example, rolling in foul-smelling substances found on walks is something that humans find hard to understand, even though we happily put on perfumes and strong-smelling creams and lotions. Walking around and around in a tight circle to flatten the place where they have chosen to lie down, even if that is a bare floor or carpet, is another behavior that puzzles human owners, although it would have made perfect sense to a dog living in the wild. This book shows photographs of many of these

Dogs are similar to us in many ways, and many anxiously await the return of loved ones when they are left alone.

apparently confusing behaviors and explains what is really going on when the reasons are not so obvious.

Many of the behaviors that are unacceptable to owners arise from a dog's inherited drives to maintain the body and keep fit. In particular, behavior that is designed to help dogs find and kill prey to eat often gets our pet dogs into trouble. Most owners can understand why their dogs like to chase, but their dog's love of chasing inappropriately—after joggers, cars, wheelchairs, and even their own tail—can leave humans perplexed and at a loss as to how to control their pets.

This book also celebrates the similarities we have with our dogs, particularly their sociability,

Dogs are descended from animals that scavenged for a living, and enjoy rolling in decaying carrion or feces to coat their neck region in the alluring smell.

which makes them such pleasant and rewarding companions. Although dogs share a similar desire to develop close bonds, they express their affection in different ways to us, often leaving us confused over what they are trying to say. This book explains why dogs jump up to greet us, for example, or why they carry things around when they get excited.

A dog's lack of speech is part of his charm but can also lead to difficult situations if he cannot easily express himself when he doesn't like something we do. This book helps to shed light on why dogs may become angry or aggressive and describes the warning signs to watch out for when dealing with unfamiliar dogs.

This book will answer your questions about why dogs do the peculiar, endearing, or embarrassing things that are often unacceptable from a human point of view. It will give you a greater knowledge of canine behavior so that you can be more tolerant of the things dogs want to do and create acceptable outlets for those impulses. Understanding why our dogs do what they do helps us to appreciate them more, develop a closer bond with them, and give them a better quality of life.

Social by nature and sharing many of their owners' emotions, dogs make ideal companions for active humans.

SOCIAL ETIQUETTE

Strange greetings

Dogs are highly social animals and enjoy relationships with other dogs and humans, but their ways of meeting and greeting are very different from how we would say hello. Trusted friends are greeted with exuberant enthusiasm and excitement. Even a short absence can result in a truly ecstatic greeting that is one of the characteristics of dogs that owners find most appealing. Strangers are treated with more reserve and caution and are subjected to a lot of investigation to find out if they are friend or foe.

So good to see you!

Lots of tail wagging and exuberance welcome this owner home. She has crouched down to put herself at face level with the dogs, removing the need for them to jump up to get close to her face. Excitement and frantic activity, with lots of happy tail wagging, accompany the greeting and show the importance of their human family to these dogs.

Nice to meet you.

These two dogs are relaxed about encountering other dogs, so meet nose to nose. By sniffing the breath and face of the other, they can tell a lot about their state of health, what they have been eating, and where they have been. The black dog is less at ease and raises his tail to make himself look bigger — just in case she gets difficult!

Who are you?

Sniffing bottoms may seem unpleasant to humans but it provides dogs with a valuable source of information. Their sense of smell is highly developed (see pages 38–41) and they can find out lots about a new arrival by sniffing. The bottom is a good place to start, as scent glands are located here and it is away from the head end, which may bite!

Making contact

Jumping up is a bad habit that can ruin owners' clothes or cause injury. Dogs that jump up don't mean to be naughty, however, but are trying to give their owner's face an affectionate lick. Puppies instinctively lick the mouths of other pack members in greeting. In the wild, this would result in the returning adult dogs regurgitating food they had eaten while out hunting for the pups to eat. If puppies learn that face licking and jumping up wins them attention from us, the habit may continue into adulthood.

It's you, it's you!

This puppy climbs on his young owner to reach his face. Puppies will try to lick our mouths but we usually turn away, resulting in a nose or face lick instead. The sudden proximity of the puppy's face to his own makes this boy laugh and squirm. The enhanced social contact will reward the puppy's behavior and he is likely to try it again later.

ATTENTION SEEKING

Some dogs bark at owners, jump up, pull at their clothing, and try to climb all over them. These dogs are often particularly sociable and may not be getting sufficient attention from their busy owners. In order to break these bad habits, owners need to set aside time to give their dog enough satisfying love and attention, as well as plenty of exercise and play. Once their dog's desire for attention is satisfied, owners can ignore attention-seeking behavior shown at inappropriate times.

Please love me.

This young dog lives with her mother and licks at her mouth. Unlike humans, dogs don't mind this behavior and usually only lift their heads higher if the licking becomes too persistent or if it prevents them from seeing properly. The raised paw, tail down, and ears back all signal appeasement and, in combination with the mouth licking, show that the youngster may feel she has some making up to do.

Come down a bit farther.

Jumping up can be an annoying habit from the owner's point of view, although some may unwittingly encourage it by rewarding their dog with affection when it's done, as this owner is doing. This basset has short legs but a long body and so his owner is helping to steady him while they greet each other.

Ready to play

Dogs get excited when their owners return home and will often display unexpected behavior, such as fetching a toy or tugging at clothes. This is because excitement makes them want to play their favorite game. Dogs play in various ways (see pages 26–27) and enjoy the social interaction that play brings. The most fulfilling play involves others and, although dogs will play alone, they prefer to try to entice others into a game if they can.

I'm so excited!

This dog looks up excitedly at her owner, with mouth open and face relaxed, seeking a reaction to her play-bow. Her elbows nearly touch the floor, she is ready to spring up if her invitation to play is accepted, and her tail wags. Dogs will only make this display if they feel confident and happy with their owners.

Please play with me.

Play-bows to other dogs are a clear invitation to play. The older dog is not sure he wants to play with the younger, more exuberant dog, and turns his head to signal disinterest. He has enough confidence in his communication skills to ignore the younger dog until he has made up his mind whether to play or not.

You're home!

An excited golden retriever puppy proudly carries a shoe and approaches his owners for social contact. Owners will often misinterpret such an approach, assuming the puppy is bringing the shoe as a gift for them. They extend a hand to receive it, only for the puppy to veer off in a different direction to stop them taking it.

FAVORITE GAMES

An excited dog that is full of energy will try to play his favorite game. He may race around, find an object to hold in his mouth (one of your cherished shoes, for example), chase his tail, grab at clothing for a tug-of-war game, or try to play with any other dog in the household. Overcome this behavior by providing your dog with his own toys and teaching him how to play with them. This can prevent the dog from finding his own games and objects to play with, which may result in bad habits and the destruction of precious items.

Living with children

Dogs usually cope well with new babies in the family but find it more difficult once they grow into toddlers. Teenagers are often more interested in things away from home but a strong bond developed in childhood will last during this difficult time. Dogs can be a great source of comfort to children, especially when they are troubled or lonely. Dogs and children can build strong and lasting friendships if both are brought up to understand and respect each other from an early age.

My best friend

This dog is relaxed and confident. The boy looks directly at him, so the dog shifts his gaze so that he isn't staring back. He is comfortable with being looked at and touched, but looking his friend in the eye at such a close range would make him feel uneasy. Friendships formed during these early years can be very rewarding for both parties as they mature.

It's fun playing with you!

Puppies raised with children soon learn to enjoy being with them, providing both are taught to have consideration for the other. This puppy is learning just how much fun playing with this girl can be and eagerly moves forward to catch the toy. Supervision of games will allow them both to learn to moderate their behavior and will prevent games getting out of hand.

I like our new family.

If the family dog associates a new baby with a reduction in attention to himself, he may develop negative feelings toward the baby. Continuing to give love and attention to the dog while caring for a new baby is important for the dog's sense of well-being. This is easier if the dog is well trained, like this one, so that affection can be given without disruption to the baby. The dog can then learn to accept the new addition without any jealous feelings.

Go away!

This could be a dangerous situation for the toddler, who is fast approaching a dog that is worried he may lose his toy. The dog keeps his mouth on the toy, but his eyes look towards the child. He remains in a relaxed position with his feet out to the side, but there could be trouble if the toddler touches the dog near his head.

LIVING IN A PACK

Part of the family

Dogs like to live in packs and, as humans also like to live in social groups, this trait enables them to fit well into our families. If dogs are raised with humans from an early age, they will view them as part of their social structure and will be happier with them than with members of their own species. Problems may arise if dogs are raised only with other dogs, as they will prefer canine company and may be unhappy if kept as the only dog in a human household.

I know you too well.

Two puppies from the same litter growing up in a household form very strong bonds of friendship, often to the exclusion of their owners. These two dogs are very evenly matched and enjoy playing games of strength together. Unless owners take time to separate them and teach them to play with people, these dogs may never develop a good relationship with their owners.

Good to be with you.

Well-socialized dogs love to be with us, and this dog shows his pleasure with his friendly exuberance. To be so sociable, dogs need to have had lots of pleasant encounters with humans before twelve weeks of age. Happy encounters with people before this time will establish a predisposition for friendly behavior when the dog meets humans in future.

This is fun.

The desire to join in with pack activities helps to make dogs the perfect pet for families and people who want to involve them in most aspects of their lives. Dog owners who go running or skating with their canine are often pleasantly surprised by their dog's willingness to keep just the right pace with them. This dog happily jogs along with his owner, leading the way if his human runs too slowly, but never running off completely, as the sense of purpose he shares with his owner is very strong.

Potential pack troubles

Owning more than one dog can bring unexpected problems. Pairs of dogs that grow up together from puppies can bond more strongly with each other than with their owners. The increased confidence they derive from this relationship can lead them into all sorts of trouble. Introducing a puppy to an older dog, or a newly rescued dog to an existing dog, often works out well but difficulties can still arise if their personalities and breed characteristics are not compatible.

Pester power

This puppy is trying to entice the older dog to play, but she resists. If an older dog is not sufficiently assertive to stop a youngster from pestering, a puppy will quickly learn to demand play whenever he wants and to play too roughly. He will then become very frustrated—and sometimes aggressive—when prevented from playing by a more confident dog later in life.

Let's go get 'em!

Two dogs out together without their owner will be more confident and more likely to become predatory than a dog out on his own. The influence of the pack is strong and, if these dogs find an animal to chase, they are more likely to bring it down and bite it than if each were on his own or under the control of his owner.

HE'S NOT LIKE OUR OLD DOG

Owners are often so pleased with their dog that they acquire a puppy of the same breed, hoping for the same temperament again. They are often disappointed to find that the puppy grows up to be more dog focused and uninterested in the human family members. This is because the first dog grew up in human-only society, whereas the puppy has had the other dog for companionship and thus did not need to bond with the humans in the same way.

Play with me.

The solution to pack problems is for the owner to play lots of games with his puppy. If a puppy is playing with humans, he has no need to pester other dogs in the family, nor will he learn to play inappropriate games. In addition, the puppy will learn to respond to and bond with his owners, which will keep him out of trouble later in life.

All by myself

Sociability is one of the traits that has been accentuated over the centuries by selective breeding to create dogs to work with humankind. As a result, dogs prefer to be with company and can find it very difficult to cope with isolation, unless taught to do so from an early age. This can lead to problems such as excessive vocalization, destruction, or house-soiling when the dog is left alone—all of which can be expensive, disruptive, and exasperating for owners who are not there to prevent the unwelcome behavior.

Please come back!

Dogs that are worried about being alone will bark or howl to try to call their owners home. The anxiety they feel can drive them to bark or howl continuously, hour after hour, until their owners return. Dogs like this need careful and slow training with short, then gradually longer absences, so that they learn to cope with being on their own.

This feels good.

Puppies and young dogs chew to exercise their jaws and relieve boredom. To prevent the destruction of household items, dogs need to be taught to select dog chews and strong toys for chewing, rather than furniture. The chewing of acceptable items that you have provided needs to become an established habit before you leave them with a free run of the house.

I like to be near you.

Dogs like to be close to their owners; it's a trait many owners value. However, dogs that are excessively bonded can have trouble coping when their owner is suddenly removed from their company. If their fear is great enough, they may become anxious enough to bark, cause destruction while trying to get out, or soil the house.

Shall I wait here?

Teaching puppies such as this one to wait patiently while the owner moves away and eventually passes out of sight is an important lesson. A baby gate is a good tool to use at this early stage, as the puppy is kept separate but can still see his owner. A puppy that gets used to being left alone will gradually accept periods of solitude as part of his everyday life.

Socializing with other dogs

Dogs can get along very well with other dogs providing they are introduced to them at an early age. They need to learn successful strategies for meeting and greeting other dogs on walks, as well as how to read all the body language that accompanies such encounters. Dogs that spend a lot of time with humans often ignore other dogs when out on walks, but even they need to learn what to do if another dog forces an interaction.

Do you want to be friends?

The brown dog is well socialized and friendly. She moves forward slowly, with a gently waving tail and a relaxed face and body. The collie is not so sure. He stiffens and raises his tail, holding himself high to be as impressive as possible should things become difficult. His tense face and pulled-back ears show that he is feeling ill at ease.

I'll catch you.

Chase games are a great energy release for dogs that are friendly with other dogs. They usually take it in turns to be the chaser, unless one dog definitely prefers that role. These littermates have grown up together and are evenly matched for speed and turning ability. Playing together in this way strengthens the bond between them and keeps them fit, too.

Can I have that?

Two puppies kept together in the same family have plenty of opportunity to learn about how to interact with others by playing together. However, they will also need plenty of socialization with other dogs of different breeds, temperaments, and personalities if they are to get along well with every dog they meet on a walk.

Let me squash you.

The black collie has put his paws onto the back of the Dalmatian to try to subdue her. Trying to stand with front paws on the back of another dog is rarely tolerated and often results in a fight. This Dalmatian is a friendly dog and doesn't take offense, as shown by her relaxed body and tail.

Learning to play nicely

Even if dogs have plenty of access to other dogs while growing up, they will not, necessarily, learn to play nicely with each other. If allowed to play unsupervised, puppies may play too roughly or may learn to exhibit defensive or aggressive behavior in order to compel other pups to stop. In a natural pack, older dogs will stop play before it gets out of hand. In families where more than one dog is kept, owners need to assume this role to ensure fair play.

Ouch, that hurts!

Learning how rough he can be and how hard he can bite his opponent without hurting is an important part of a puppy's play. If the bite is too hard, the other puppy will get up and move away, thus ending the game and teaching the puppy to be gentler with his jaws if he wants to keep the game going next time.

That's enough!

The smaller of these two dogs has had enough but the larger one wants to keep playing. The smaller one faces the other and barks threateningly to try to make the other one back down. This only excites the other into more vigorous play. Owners need to step in at this point to break up the game before the situation gets out of hand.

THRESHOLDS OF AGGRESSION

I'm bigger than you.

Wrestling games are often enjoyed by puppies, especially those of breeds that like physical contact. Standing over or pinning down your opponent is good practice for fighting. Owners need to make sure that they play with each puppy individually much more than each puppy plays with his littermate to ensure that they develop a good relationship with each puppy and stay in control of the pack.

Owners are often surprised when their gentle puppy becomes aggressive towards other dogs. Dogs of different breeds have varying thresholds of aggression. Most terriers are very quick to use aggression, for example, whereas hounds are very laid back and only resort to aggression if necessary. Owners planning to purchase a puppy need to investigate carefully what the ancestors of the puppy were originally bred for, as well as looking carefully at the temperaments of the parents and grandparents.

HUMAN FRIENDS

Interaction with owners

Dogs generally enjoy good relationships with their owners and many of their social behaviors fit in well with ours. People who like dogs universally recognize the happy, tail-wagging greeting and many dogs enjoy being stroked and cuddled by their owners. Dogs do not naturally touch or hug to show affection, however, and need to be taught that this is our way of showing affection. Owners, likewise, need to learn the signals that tell them whether their dog is at ease and friendly, or not.

I like to be near you.

There is a trusting and close relationship between this dog and his owner, allowing the dog to enjoy the close contact. By leaning toward the dog and looking down at his face, she causes this sensitive dog to be a little bit less at ease, as shown by his open mouth, ears drawn back a little, and his head turned away from her.

Feels so good

To help them learn to appreciate our displays of physical affection, puppies must be handled from an early age. This puppy is completely at ease with his young friend and has fallen asleep while she touches his neck. This happy relaxation is not possible in a puppy that is worried about contact with people; in that case he would have moved away or curled up tightly to protect himself.

Hello to you, too!

Someone familiar to this dog has just spoken to him, resulting in a big wag of his tail, his ears being pulled down and slightly back, and his relaxed face showing the classic "I'm pleased to see you" expression. A wagging tail means a dog is excited and, although this is a friendly wag, a stiff tail wag with different facial expressions could signal fear and aggression.

Not too close

Not all dogs feel comfortable when people touch and hold them. Some may not have been familiarized with human handling as puppies, and some may have had bad experiences that have made them apprehensive about what may come next. If we ignore or fail to recognize his signals of anxiety, a dog can reach a point where he feels the need to become aggressive in order to get away or be left alone. Understanding these signals and helping him to regain trust in humans is essential to successful handling.

Let me go.

This dog does not want to interact with or come any closer to his owner. The owner is trying to pull him toward him, but the dog resists. He turns his head and ignores his owner, deliberately staring in a different direction. He is not afraid, but something is very wrong with the relationship between these two.

Don't hurt me.

Although the examination is gentle, this dog is not happy being touched by a stranger. Her tail is clamped down between her legs to keep it safe, her body is rigid, and she shows her concern through her tense face and ears pinned back against her head. This sensitive dog could have had a bad experience in the past, but limited early contact with people is the more likely cause of this reaction.

Leave me alone.

A display of teeth and a piercing stare is a clear message to stop — or else! Although this dog is lying down, it is likely she has had no choice in the matter, and is now very concerned that she will be hurt. Her tail is clamped between her legs, she is tense, and her eyelids have opened wide, revealing the whites of her eyes.

FEELING VULNERABLE

Many owners find it difficult to understand why their dog becomes aggressive when they mean no harm. Looking at it from the dog's point of view, however, reveals how vulnerable the dog is in the relationship, with limited means of communication and with no choice in the decisions made by his owner. To make him feel less vulnerable, it is important to be considerate and thoughtful in our dealings with him and to learn to read and respond to his body-language signals.

That's weird!

Dogs are like us in so many ways that it is easy to forget that they are a completely different species. They see life from a different point of view and have bodies that are similar to but very unlike ours. For this reason, they may exhibit behaviors that seem peculiar to us and that appear to have no purpose, such as licking our skin or scratching with a hind leg when we scratch them in a ticklish spot.

Can I join in?

Pushing in while owners cuddle, sit, or lie together is usually a ploy to become the center of attention again. Some strong-willed dogs that have a pathological need for attention may even become aggressive when owners show affection to each other instead of to them.

Oooh, right there!

Early dogs that descended from wolves and lived around human settlements may have had many parasites, as do dogs living in similar conditions today. Scratching is one way to remove the worst offenders and there are many places on a dog's body where gentle tickling, such as this dog is receiving, can induce a full-scale scratching movement in the hind legs.

A good licking

Dogs may lick our skin for many different reasons, but it's usually because they like the taste. This dog is licking the forearm of his owner, where scent of the sweat on the skin may have attracted him. Dogs may also like to lick perfume and other strong scents from our skin, and some dogs may learn to lick hands and feet to get attention from their owners.

My comforter

Many puppies suck and chew their bedding while settling down to sleep. This is most common in puppies that were removed early from their mother and could be a way of replacing the comforting feeling of suckling. Some grow out of it, while other dogs will do it all their lives. It is a harmless activity, provided it is not done to excess.

Listen to me

Dogs make a range of sounds, with yips, cries, whines, and howls being just some of the ways they use to communicate with us and other dogs. Unless barking has become a bad habit, however, dogs are usually silent, preferring to communicate using their rich repertoire of body language rather than with noises as we do. In order to please us, they will try to learn many of our spoken words and noise patterns, but they often respond more naturally and readily to our movements and gestures.

Throw it, throw it!

Previous experience has taught this Labrador that barking causes his owners to throw the ball for him more quickly. Labradors love to swim and his wagging tail shows he is excited about the prospect of jumping into the water to fetch his toy. Rewarding his barking with a throw of the toy will make him more likely to bark again in the future.

Aaaaaaaahhoooo!

Howling is an effective way for our dog's ancestors, the wolves, to communicate with other members of the pack over a long distance. Some dogs still do this, especially when left alone or when they hear two-tone sounds that stimulate this ancient behavior. Many dogs are set off by sirens, mouth organs, certain tunes, or people singing.

Are you ready to play?

This basset hound jumps around and barks excitedly, trying to hurry his owner into playing a game or going for a walk. Barking with excitement is more common in dogs that live a relatively quiet life and have few outings. Each event can then produce great excitement and stimulation, which is expressed by the dog in movement and barking.

Quiet, please.

Teaching puppies not to bark is essential if you want them to be quiet later in life. This puppy receives an early lesson and is learning that a finger held up in front of the face means "be quiet." Some breeds of dog have been bred as watchdogs in which a willingness to bark is essential; they will need more training to be quiet than naturally quieter breeds.

SPECIAL POWERS

Led by the nose

A dog's extraordinary sense of smell is responsible for some of the stranger or more "disgusting" things that dogs sometimes do. The surface area of a dog's nose used for scent detection is fourteen times greater than a human's and dogs also have a much larger area of the brain devoted to smells than we do. This enables dogs to detect minute traces of odor and to distinguish subtle differences between scents in a way that we find hard to imagine.

I was here.

Dogs will scratch up the ground with their feet if they want to leave a message to other dogs that they were in the territory. This usually happens after they have marked the place with urine or feces. The glands between the toes leave additional smells on the ground as they rake—an unmistakable scent mark for others.

Canine graffiti

Once mature, male dogs will lift their hind leg when urinating. This allows them to leave a urine scent mark on trees and bushes just at the height of a dog's nose to advertise their presence to others. These scent marks are usually put on top of urine marks left by other dogs, and thus serve as an effective community notice-board for the dogs in the same neighborhood.

I'll smell so good!

Many dogs like to roll in mucky substances, such as decaying bodies and feces. This dog has found part of a decaying mouse on the grass and blissfully rubs it around his neck as if putting on expensive perfume. Scavenging was once an important source of food and it could be that they just enjoy the aroma in the same way that we like the smell of flowers.

Every sniff tells a story

Sniffing at scents is a dog's equivalent of reading a gossip magazine. It provides a rich source of information and explains why they are so keen to sniff, sometimes in places that are not considered polite by humans. Dogs can tell who you are, your state of health, and what you had for dinner all from just one sniff.

Let me smell your bottom.

It may seem distasteful to us, but it makes perfect sense for the larger dog to want to sniff the area where the other dog's anal glands are located. These glands provide a distinct personal scent for each dog, the equivalent of a person's name and facial features, as well as other clues such as state of health, sexual status, age, and even what the other dog has eaten.

Are you safe?

Sniffing at our hands can help a dog find out a lot about us, including whether we are scared. Sweat glands in our palms will exude chemicals associated with fear if we are anxious. This dog is worried about contact with humans and approaches cautiously, with her ears back and tail down. Any adverse scents will cause her to back off and end the interaction.

I'm not too sure about you.

Bottom sniffing provides more information than nose sniffing but it requires closer proximity. Some dogs are not comfortable with this. The beagle tucks her tail down and keeps her body facing the larger dog so she cannot come too close. The large dog is relaxed and easy-going, and contents herself with sniffing the beagle's nose for now, rather than pushing to get closer.

Walking and sniffing

Dogs find scents left by other dogs fascinating. The dog on the left is kept busy while the other dogs get to know each other. Dogs sometimes sniff intently like this rather than get involved in something they find scary, such as meeting other dogs. This dog, however, is not worried, as shown by his raised tail and relaxed body.

Finding food

The ancestors of the dog probably obtained a lot of their food by scavenging, so we shouldn't be surprised if our pet dogs have retained this important instinct. Less understandable is their desire to eat things that we would consider repellent, such as grass, sticks, feces, and decaying material. But, for dogs, these items can be a good source of nutrients and seem to be relished in the same way that we would enjoy an unusual snack or treat.

It's a feast!

Taking food whenever they could get it would have been a successful strategy for our dogs' ancestors. Dogs like this one have no conscience about taking food from their owner's plate or stealing food that doesn't belong to them. His survival instinct is telling him to make the most of it while he can because the opportunity may not come again.

Good medicine

Some dogs, like this one, feel the need to eat grass periodically. Dogs' jaws move only up and down, not side to side like a cow's, so grass eating is relatively difficult for them. Dogs eat grass when they feel the need to be sick, and also sometimes when they need it to aid their digestion in some way.

Look what I've found!

Dogs are attracted to the smell of decaying flesh that we would find disgusting. This dog has found a rare prize of a dead fish and carries it proudly onto the shore. Their strong stomach acids enable them to digest small quantities without becoming ill, if they can eat their find quickly before their owner makes them drop it.

Powers of sound and vision

Dogs' amazing hearing accounts for behavior that often astounds humans, such as the way they get ready to greet owners long before they have arrived home, or respond to sounds in the ultrasonic range, such as those of small prey animals or "silent" dog whistles. Dogs can hear sounds up to four times farther away than we can and will hear close-up noises more acutely. Dogs also have a remarkable ability to see in low light levels. They can see in color, but are limited to yellows and blues.

Mobile ears

This dog has raised his ears and turned his head to try to identify exactly where the sound is coming from. The difference in the time it takes for the sound to reach each ear will allow his brain to locate the source of the sound with pinpoint accuracy. This ability allows dogs to locate small prey animals in tall grass so they can be caught with the first pounce.

They'll be home soon.

Many dogs begin waiting by the window or door just before their owners arrive home. Scientists are divided on whether this is due to their super powerful hearing, which can detect the sounds of the owner's arrival long before a human observer can, or whether they have an extra "sixth" sense, perhaps telepathy, that tells them when their owner is about to return.

Night vision

Dogs can see in much dimmer light conditions than we can. This allows them to speed off into apparent darkness without crashing into trees, an ability that often amazes their owners. Their night vision is due to a reflective membrane in their eyes that traps light and allows them to see more clearly—useful for hunting prey that is only active at dawn and dusk.

SURVIVAL STRATEGIES

Perceiving threats

Staying safe is a matter that both dogs and humans take very seriously. However, dogs often see a threat where we would not. This leads to situations where a dog may bark or become aggressive unexpectedly. Dogs are particularly likely to guard boundaries and entry/exit points to prevent a threat from coming onto their territory, particularly if they feel a person is doing something suspicious — such as making a noise at the door.

Stay out!

This Labrador guards his territory by barking while standing close to the gate, his stiffly wagging tail displaying his excitement. His weight is evenly distributed on all four feet, showing that he has no intention of running away if challenged, although this may change if the threat becomes more frightening. Only his backward-facing ears shows that he is fearful.

Keep away!

Delivery people are often targeted by dogs because they come to the property boundary, do something disruptive such as ringing the doorbell, and, when barked at, go away again. This dog barks confidently to try to remove the threat to the property, raising his tail and watching to see if his efforts are successful.

This is my yard!

Caught out in the open with no barrier, this dog is brave enough to challenge the intruder. He makes himself look large by putting his tail up and standing tall. He barks threateningly, planting his front feet squarely to show that he means business. His ears are halfway between being pinned back for protection and moving forward to display his strength during his threat display.

Hands off!

Some dogs do not trust humans implicitly and find it difficult to accept that they mean them no harm. This can lead to upsetting encounters for people who do not know how to read warning signs and who persist in their approach. Problems are exacerbated if the person tries to touch the dog, either to groom it or to comfort it. If warning signs are ignored or misread, the dog may feel he has no choice but to bite to keep himself safe from this perceived threat.

Don't touch me!

This dog makes it clear that he is not happy to be approached, despite the owner's persistence. Dogs often view their bed as a safe haven and are quick to defend the area if they feel threatened. This dog's protruding tongue, raised lips, and eye slightly turned to the left shows that he is guarding something in his bed that he doesn't want taken away.

Please don't.

Grooming can be a stressful experience for dogs, especially if the owner is rough or inconsiderate, or gets upset with the dog for noncompliance. This dog puts his ears back, shows the whites of his eyes, and looks worried, using his paws to try to prevent his owner from brushing him. He needs careful desensitization to help him to learn to accept gentle grooming.

Feels good!

Getting used to being groomed gently at an early age can help to build trust and will result in a dog that loves to be brushed. This puppy is relaxed and content, having been familiarized with both brushing and lying still on a table while it happens. When this dog grows larger, his trusting nature will make it easy for his owner to keep his coat in good condition.

Aggression in close quarters

A small space is easily defended and dogs that are worried about people are often aggressive in cars and kennels or when they feel cornered. Dogs that are unable to run away, when they are on a leash, for example, will often use aggression to keep threats at bay. Although we may not see people or other dogs as a threat, dogs that are lacking in socialization or who have had bad experiences may do so, and may feel they need to resort to aggression to keep themselves safe.

I'm on guard!

Cars provide small, defendable spaces that can be easily guarded. A dog in a confined space is trapped and has nowhere to run. This dog doesn't understand that the car doors are locked and so barks vigorously to deter intruders. A hard stare, teeth on display, and an explosive series of barks will keep most threats away.

Nice to meet you.

To prevent aggression, it is important that puppies meet, and have pleasant encounters with, as wide a range of people and other animals as possible during their first years. In particular, the socialization period of a puppy's life, from three to sixteen weeks, is a time when puppies are particularly sensitive to developing good relationships, and every effort should be made to give puppies happy encounters during that time.

Move away—or else!

Dogs will often put on a threat display to try to make another dog or person go away. This dog cannot run or move far away. Previous experience has taught her to act aggressively to keep herself safe. Although she leans forward with bared teeth, a hard stare, and growling, her pulled-back ears and low tail show that she is very fearful.

Don't come any closer!

This dog is worried about the person approaching his kennel and lets him know he is prepared to use aggression if he comes any closer. The bared teeth, hard stare, and growl make his warning very clear. Dogs that live outside like this away from human contact find it difficult to learn to trust people and realize that they mean no harm.

Aggression toward other dogs

Owners often find it difficult to understand why their dogs are aggressive to other dogs and may punish them, which will just make the problem worse. Dogs are usually aggressive to other dogs if they have had limited socialization or bad experiences with them, making them anxious about what another dog might do when they meet. Even if their fears are unfounded, these dogs will react aggressively to try to keep themselves safe, with enough force to make the other dog back away.

Go away now!

The German shepherd dog cannot cope with this playful Labrador and gives a threat display to try to get him to back off. His tail is lowered and he moves forward barking loudly and displaying his teeth. His back legs are very weak and he doesn't want to risk the pain of even a playful encounter with another dog.

Keep back, I'm really scared now!

The red collie is worried about what the other collie may do to him and tucks his tail down, puts his weight on his back legs ready to run, and turns to face her, showing his teeth with a direct stare and aggressive barking. The playful collie continues to try to make him run, carefully keeping her distance while goading him.

I'm really mad at you!

Arousal levels during an extended play session have risen until they boiled over into aggression. This is common in terriers, which have quick, reactive temperaments. The arousal brought on by exuberant physical play develops until it takes only a very small indiscretion to make the other dog angry. Once one is annoyed, it quickly develops into a big argument.

I'll get you!

The small dog's fast running has made the larger dog defensive. He lunges forward in a mock attack, with tail up and the hackles along his back raised. The small dog leaps away, pulling back his ears to keep them safe and giving a surprised bark as he does so. All the excitement has caused the dog on the right to raise his tail.

Learning aggression

Owners are often surprised and upset when their dog becomes aggressive to other dogs. Puppies are not born aggressive, but learn to use aggression through inappropriate play or bad experiences with other dogs. Sometimes, they may have been frightened by other dogs during puppyhood, but do not acquire the confidence to show aggression until they begin to mature into adults. Shy puppies that lack good exposure to friendly dogs during early puppyhood learn to use aggression more easily than others.

Get off me!

These puppies have played together for too long and are getting tired and irritable with each other. Older dogs in a pack will stop puppies playing for too long to avoid things reaching this point, and owners should do the same, breaking up play sessions to prevent any disputes and showing them how to play nicely using games with toys.

Making friends

To ensure that puppies grow into adult dogs that will be friendly toward other dogs, they need to meet and have lots of pleasant encounters with other dogs and puppies as they go through puppyhood. Games with others need to be supervised to ensure that puppies are learning to play nicely and play should be stopped if it gets too rough.

Puppies that are allowed to play roughly with other dogs will grow up thinking this is acceptable. Later, when they try to play roughly with dogs that are less tolerant, they may find themselves on the receiving end of an aggressive response. If this happens several times, the puppy may then learn to be aggressive as well as rough when meeting other dogs. To break this chain of learned responses, puppy play needs to be carefully controlled by owners to ensure it remains gentle and acceptable.

Stop that

Very young puppies will readily move closer. This collie cannot cope with this puppy's approach and is being aggressive to stop it. The puppy cowers down in a submissive posture, getting close to the floor and rolling slightly to show that he means no harm. The puppy will remember this response and as a result be more likely to use aggression himself when he is older.

Signs of unease

Dogs give clear visible signals when they are uneasy and worried. They may yawn, raise a paw, or lick their nose, as well as show displacement activities, such as sniffing grass or scratching. If these signs are not seen or understood by owners and they continue to pressure their dog, he will be forced to take more drastic action to feel safe. Learning to read the early warning signs can prevent a lot of upset and help the dog to feel more comfortable in his world.

I'm not comfortable.

Dogs yawn for several reasons, often because they are anxious rather than because they are tired. This dog is being pressured to lie down for the photo. His body is tense and he is ready to spring up if he needs to. He shows his concern with pulled back ears, a tense face, and a big yawn.

Hmm, I'm not sure.

Uneasy about being made to sit in front of this girl who stares and shows her teeth, this pointer looks worried, turns her head slowly to the side to try to disengage from the encounter, and raises her front paw off the ground. Humans frequently misinterpret this gesture, thinking that the dog wants to shake hands and may try to hold the paw.

Feeling the pressure

The brown dog is anxious about the other dog's approach so she licks her nose and raises her paw. These are not necessarily signals made for the other dog to read, but are done to make herself feel better. A dog or a person who is skilled in interactions with dogs will read these signs and reduce the pressure of the encounter.

I'm really worried now.

Nose licking of this magnitude is a sure sign that this dog feels anxious and uncomfortable with the situation. Her ears are laid back and the tension shows in her face. Nose licking also has a nose-cleaning function, but anxious dogs will repeatedly flick out their tongues or lick their lips and nose until the danger is passed.

Warning signals

Dogs are often blamed for biting unexpectedly, seemingly with no warning. In fact, they often give many signals that all is not well before resorting to aggression. They cannot ask us to move away or write us a note. Often they are completely captive in a given situation and cannot move away to avoid a threat. Their body language clearly shows they are unhappy, however, and if owners can learn to read these signals, they can help their dog out of his difficulty.

Leave me alone.

This patient Weimaraner is signaling that she is not happy with the baby's attentions. She is being asked to sit and stay still, but her eyes look pleadingly at the owner to see if she can move away without getting into trouble. Her ears are back and down, her tongue is flicking out, and she leans away from the baby.

Owners often find it difficult to know what their dog is thinking, especially if they are new to dog ownership. Interpreting the signals and signs that reveal a dog's mood can be hard unless you have plenty of experience. To learn more about your dog, watch his ears, tail, face, and body postures in different situations and try to work out how he's feeling. Observations such as these will lead to a better and quicker interpretation of his emotions.

I'm getting ready to bite!

Hands coming down from above can seem very threatening to fearful dogs, especially those that are on a lead and cannot move away. This dog shows his tension with pulled-back ears, a worried face, and a stiffened body. The direct stare and the stiff, wagging tail signal that this dog has the confidence to take things further if necessary.

Please get off me!

Dogs don't always like hugs as much as we do. This dog turns his head away from the attention and appears to be coping, but his black coat makes it difficult to read what he is thinking. Dogs have to make a lot of effort to cool down by panting on a hot day and this can make them irritable.

Appeasement

When dogs are worried, they can choose from four options
to help them feel safe again: they can run away, freeze,
fight, or appease. Appeasement is a strategy that is often
used by puppies and young dogs, as well as those who
are lacking in confidence. Appeasement can be shown by
a range of behaviors, including lip licking, paw raising,
holding the head down, and rolling over, all of which are
designed to demonstrate a lack of threat to an aggressor.

You are so important.

The older female assumes a regal bearing
in the presence of this lively young puppy.
Seeing her display of assertiveness, the young
puppy sits close and gets ready to lick her
lips. The puppy is relaxed but her held-back
ears signal that she is not completely sure
of her welcome and is ready with an
appeasement gesture if she gets told off.

Don't hurt me!

The white dog's strategy for dealing with other dogs that she regards as a threat is to lie down, roll over, and keep still. In this position, she is very vulnerable but, in doing so, she is signaling strongly that she is not a threat. This tactic works with most dogs and they leave her alone.

Tickle my tummy.

Rolling over may start out as a way of diffusing a stressful situation for a puppy, but they rapidly learn that this position brings attention from humans. This dog is relaxed and happy, and has rolled over onto his back to solicit attention. Waving paws can be used to encourage even the most reluctant human to give some fuss and attention.

Freeze or flight

Keeping very still or running away are other strategies used by frightened dogs to help make them feel safer. Both of these strategies can be employed successfully depending on the circumstances, and both are better than using aggression, as there is less likelihood of provoking more aggression from the other dog. Freezing can reduce the defensiveness of the other dog, while running away can get a dog out of danger quickly.

Whoa there!

This collie has decided that lying down and keeping still is a good way to placate the barking pointer. Her pinned-back ears and big eyes show her alarm, but she holds her ground. The pointer has approached but is now not too sure and barks at her in an effort to let her know not to rush at him when she gets up.

I'm just going over here.

The fawn-colored dog has puffed herself up to make herself look big, raising her tail and walking stiffly with a tense body. The dog on the left has seen these warning signals and is moving slowly away, a paw at a time. He also raises his tail to show he will not be bullied, and keeps an eye on her, just in case.

I'm going!

Running away is a good option if snapping jaws may harm you. This is just play and neither dog means to hurt the other. Even so, as the Doberman launches a play-biting attack, the black dog moves away fast, keeping himself safe. He turns his head to watch her as he does so to see how close she is getting.

Gotta get outta here!

Dogs that do not feel safe will often run to a place where they do. It is common to find dogs have escaped from gardens or enclosures during thunderstorms or fireworks and have run away to hide in safety. Sometimes they run in a blind panic and are at risk of being injured by cars, or run such a distance that they get lost.

THRILL OF THE CHASE

Ancient instincts

Although pet dogs no longer need to hunt to provide their own food, they still retain many hunting instincts. This can lead to exasperation for owners when their dog forever wants to hunt or chase. In addition, keeping fit and active was important to our dogs' ancestors, particularly those bred to work. Many modern dogs still have the energy and stamina to keep going all day, which can lead to problems when the dog finds himself confined to the house.

On the trail

With his incredible sense of smell, a dog can follow the scent trail of skin cells and disturbed earth left by another animal that may have passed in that direction many hours ago. Hounds and other dogs bred to hunt, such as this Great Dane, can become fixated on following trails when outside and can be very difficult to control on walks.

It's here somewhere!

Hunting can become an obsession, especially after one or two exciting chases. Whether it's chasing squirrels in the park or scaring rabbits in a field, it's difficult to compete with the thrill of a hunt. This young dog is learning to enjoy hunting and, unless she is restricted and taught to play with toys instead, her owners may have trouble controlling her as she matures.

Where is it?

Digging up a burrow and trying to catch the animal that made it is a fairly harmless pastime (though it can be destructive in the garden), as the animal is long gone. The residual smell of the animal and the soft earth encourage this energetic young dog to dig. Some dogs really enjoy this and, even though they never catch anything, the sheer enjoyment of the physical activity of digging encourages them to do it again and again.

NATURAL HUNTERS

The genes that give our dogs their instinctive desire to catch live prey come from their parents, so the hunting instinct is hardwired to a lesser or greater extent depending on the breed. This instinct is so strong that we need to teach puppies to get excitement from playing with toys early in their lives, and not give them the opportunity to learn to hunt.

Closing in on prey

Stalking is a natural behavior that allows dogs to approach their prey with care. It consists of watching the prey in a low, still posture, while creeping slowly closer. It is an instinctive action that is not taught and it is not related to how hungry the dog is. Dogs will stalk for fun and frequently get into trouble with their owners for stalking inappropriate prey animals, such as other small pets, birds, or sheep.

Slowly does it.

Border collies have been bred for generations to accentuate the stalk and chase parts of their behavioral repertoires. This collie is moving slowly toward a flock of sheep under the command of the shepherd. If no sheep are available, collies will stalk anything that moves, even leaves moving in the wind.

Let me come closer.

The slow stalking movement and intense stare from the forward-facing eyes of this collie have alarmed the chicken, which senses danger. A dog's instincts can be reined in if they are trained from an early age, but there is always a chance that their instincts will overcome any training, especially if they get very close to a prey animal or if left alone.

You look tasty.

This may look innocent, but the dog's desire to hunt is strong. Small pets are perfect-sized prey for a dog and there will be a strong temptation to catch and kill. This dog has learned that it is not possible to catch the hamster when it is in its cage, but the movements it makes are still fascinating.

Catch me if you can

Chasing other animals is part of natural hunting behavior and this instinct has been accentuated in many breeds used for hunting and herding. Owners often expect their dogs to know that this is unacceptable and are upset when it happens unexpectedly. Allowing your dog to chase is unpleasant and frightening for the chased animal and can cause accidents. Chasing needs to be diverted into games with toys, and dogs need to be trained not to chase inappropriately.

You do strange things.

This young puppy is learning that cats and kittens play in a very different way from dogs. To ensure that puppies grow up to be well behaved with other animals, they need to have good encounters with them, and be prevented from chasing them throughout their early life.

I'll stop you!

German shepherd dogs were bred to herd sheep and this fast-moving horse seems like a good substitute. The dog is enjoying the chase and has moved around in front to turn and slow the horse down. The horse can use both front and back feet as weapons to defend itself, something that may come as a painful surprise to the unsuspecting dog.

This is fun!

Owners are often surprised that their dog, such a gentle and loving animal at home with the children and even the pet cat, will chase, bite, and even kill livestock if given the chance. Chase behavior is hardwired into many dogs via their genes and, if given the opportunity, many will thoroughly enjoy harassing sheep and livestock to the point of exhaustion.

THE PREDATORY SEQUENCE

Chasing is just part of the predatory sequence used by dogs in the wild for hunting: track–stalk–chase–pounce/bite–shake/kill–consume–retrieve excess–bury excess. Selective breeding has accentuated specific parts of this sequence in different breeds, such as shake/kill in terriers, chase in herding dogs, and consume–retrieve in gundogs. Learn about your dog's genetic instincts and you'll understand why he enjoys doing what he does naturally.

Keep on runnin'

The inappropriate chasing of joggers, cyclists, cars, and anything else fast moving can be problematic for owners once their dog is in full flight after the moving object. It can cause accidents and injury to both the dog and whoever is being chased. Most dogs just want to chase, but some dogs will also bite out of excitement once they catch up with their quarry or may bite defensively if they have been punished for chasing in the past.

Going to get you!

Chasing cyclists is great fun for dogs, as they move fast and provide a good long chase before they stop. This dog is really enjoying himself and will have no remorse afterwards, even if he causes the cyclist to crash. To prevent this behavior in future, he needs to be taught to play more appropriate chase games with toys instead.

Gotcha!

This dog has caught the object of its chase and has made a grab for the jogger's clothes. Joggers may lash out to try to scare dogs away and this can predispose dogs to act defensively next time they "catch" a jogger. Terriers and other breeds that quickly become highly aroused may bite out of excitement when they catch up, but usually do so from behind.

Can't catch it!

Some dogs live in such a barren environment that the only thing that moves is their tail. Chasing their tail quickly becomes a habit, especially if started in puppyhood, and can turn into an obsession, developing the muscles more strongly on one side of the body than the other, as the dog constantly turns in the same direction.

Chasing objects

Chasing is such fun for our dogs that it is best to provide an outlet for this desire by teaching them to play with toys. Not only does this prevent unwanted or dangerous chases, but it also helps to bond them to us so that they want to be with us more than they want to chase inappropriately. Some dogs enjoy possessing the object they capture after a chase just as much as the chase itself and may be unwilling to surrender it.

Got it!

A plastic disk is a good chase game as, if thrown well, the toy floats just above the surface of the ground, giving the dog a good chase and then the satisfaction of catching it before it hits the ground. Once they have learned how to do this, many dogs love the game so much that they will run after a plastic disk again and again.

I can just reach it!

German shepherd dogs such as this one were bred to herd sheep. In the absence of a flock or games with toys they will make their own games where they can. This dog chases the washing that is going around on the clothesline in the wind, grabbing it when it comes within range.

Keep still.

Habits formed during puppyhood will last a lifetime. This puppy is learning how to chase and catch a ball. If the owners also teach the puppy to retrieve, they can develop a fun game that will use up their dog's energy—as well as its drive to chase—for the rest of its life, thus helping to prevent it getting into trouble with inappropriate chases.

Catch-and-kill games

For our dog's ancestors—the wolves—chasing would be followed by grabbing, shaking, and biting to bring down and kill prey. A whole pack is needed to bring large prey down, but small animals such as mice and rabbits require stealth and a well-aimed pounce to stun them, ready for the dispatch. Dogs often play games that practice these skills, even though they may not be needed, especially the terriers that were specially bred to catch and kill vermin.

This sounds exciting.

Squeaky toys are exciting for some dogs, as they make a squeal like a prey animal when squeezed. This puppy is learning how much fun they can be, although the toy is a little large for its mouth and hard to squeeze. Once the squeaker is broken, a dog that had enjoyed the toy will often show no further interest in it.

I can pounce!

This puppy practices the pounce, raising the front feet off the ground ready to slam them down on the ball. His inexperience means that he will fall far short of the target and, if the ball had been a real prey animal, he would have gone hungry. With practice, he will get better until he can pounce accurately.

Going to bite you!

A more accurate pounce brings this Yorkshire terrier down on target, the momentum of the pounce keeping her back legs off the ground. She has opened her mouth ready to bite the toy so it doesn't get away. Dogs of this breed were originally bred to catch rats on farms, so their desire to play catch-and-kill games with toys is strong.

So much energy

Many domestic dogs are descended from working dogs that were required to be active and fit enough to run all day. Since many owners' lives are now quite sedentary and dogs are expected to sleep while their owners are out at work, using up a dog's physical and mental energy can be quite a challenge, especially when the dog is young. Unwelcome behavior, such as pulling on the lead or running off, can arise when the dog is desperate to use up this energy in any way he can.

I've gone crazy!

Racing as fast as possible in small circles is a great way to use up excess energy. Dogs often do this when they get excited and the behavior is more common in puppies and young dogs. They tuck their tail underneath their body, put their ears back, and run around and around, in and out of obstacles, at high speed.

Must run faster!

Flat-out running uses up energy quickly. This dog is in full flight after a toy and has a body that allows him to flex for maximum speed. Teaching dogs to come back when called is essential, as they can then be allowed to run freely to use up energy in a way that would not be possible if they were always on a lead.

I like to be with you.

This puppy is learning to enjoy walking next to his owner and finds that she will stop if he gets ahead or tries to pull on the lead. Early lessons like this, while the puppy is still young and relatively slow, establish good habits and help ensure that he will not pull on the lead when older.

Got to get there quicker.

Humans walk at a very slow speed compared with how fast a dog can trot. Since trotting would be a dog's preferred speed on leaving the house, they try to make us move faster by pulling us with them. This is uncomfortable for us, particularly if the dog is large, so we need to teach dogs to be patient and to slow down.

BEING POSSESSIVE

Keeping food safe

Dogs will naturally guard edible items from us and other dogs. This can lead to conflict with owners who often use punishment to stop it, leading to an escalation of aggression. The ancestors of our pet dogs lived in times when food was in short supply and guarding food from others was important for survival. It is not surprising, therefore, that our present-day dogs also have a protective nature and have no desire to share, even if this is upsetting for us.

It's mine, back off!

The direct stare, bared teeth, and loud growl will leave an approaching person in no doubt that this dog means business. Further approaches are likely to result in a hard bite to force a retreat. It would not be sensible to proceed so is better to leave this dog with his bone and work on the problem later, seeking help from a professional if necessary.

Although guarding food is a natural behavior, it is an unacceptable response for pet dogs and can be dangerous, especially for children. It is important to teach puppies from an early age that human hands come to give, not take. This is easily done by offering a tasty treat for moving away from food, feeding the treat while taking away the food, and giving the food back immediately afterwards.

I'd like that instead.

This puppy is offered a tasty treat and is happy to leave her dinner to take it. Lessons such as this early in life will teach her that humans have no interest in her food and are not likely to take it away. Instead, she will find that they usually bring something that tastes better than the normal food and will learn to welcome their arrival.

I told you to leave it!

The older dog with the bone has warned this puppy not to come closer, probably with a stiffened posture and lifted lips, but the puppy is too young to understand. As a result the older dog has escalated the threat, with a head lunge, protruding tongue, and growl aimed in the puppy's direction, causing him to take avoiding action.

Possessive games

Dogs love to play tug-of-war games and really enjoy the competition to see who is stronger. Puppies will play this type of game with their littermates and it is good practice for the day when they may need to seriously compete with others for food. For our well-fed pets, tug-of-war is useful for keeping fit and having fun. These games can become rough, however, so we need to teach them how to play nicely during puppyhood.

Pull, pull!

A lightweight human is no match for a large dog with a low center of gravity. This dog causes her human to lean back to make the game more even. Trust is needed since, if the dog lets go suddenly, her owner will fall. Some dogs are more vigorous in play and may twist or shake a toy to force the human to let go.

Mind my teeth.

This puppy is enjoying the competition for the toy and pulls hard to try to win. Tug-of-war needs to be played gently with young puppies while they lose their baby teeth and their adult teeth develop. This is a good time to teach the rules of the game, such as to let go when asked, to bite only the toy rather than human fingers, and to calm down when overexcited.

This is mine!

For some dogs, possession of toys is really important and they don't like giving them up. This puppy is watching carefully to see if she needs to run away as her owner tries to grab her toy. Since dogs are usually faster and more agile than us, we need to teach our dogs to bring their toys to us, perhaps in exchange for treats.

Let's have a game

Puppies that enjoy tug-of-war games need to be taught how to play this game using toys only. Otherwise they may try to get their humans to play by tugging on sleeves, trouser legs, shoelaces, or anything loose. Bad habits can quickly develop if dogs are allowed to jump up and grab at clothing to try to play their favourite game.

The desire to dig

Digging to bury bones is a very natural behavior in dogs and one which would have allowed their ancestors to save excess food for another day. Owners do not always appreciate their dogs' digging efforts, however, especially when they dig in a prized flower bed or make holes in the lawn. Understanding the desire of dogs to dig and teaching them to use specially appointed places with verbal encouragement and by burying items there that a dog will enjoy finding can be a good solution.

I'll just put this here.

Any excess food can be stored underground where it will be safe from flies and other animals that would like to eat it. Although this rawhide chew made from animal skin is unlikely to attract flies and there are no other animals to steal it, the Labrador is responding to ancient drives and is burying it anyway.

Digging is fun!

Digging in water is common and often done by dogs that have lots of energy. It has little to do with burying food, but the action is the same and is enjoyed for its own sake. In addition, lots of water droplets are thrown up, which many dogs enjoy trying to catch, making this energetic game very worthwhile.

I know it's here somewhere.

Finding buried food is not usually a priority for dogs that like to dig. Hungry dogs may revisit previously dug sites, but most well-fed pet dogs come across buried bones by accident rather than by deliberately digging in the right place. Terriers were selectively bred to dig out prey and many dig for fun as well as the excitement of catching prey animals.

GETTING COMFORTABLE

The urge to chew

Strong teeth and jaws are needed for catching prey and then for dismembering it and pulverizing bones to obtain the correct nutrients. Although our pet dogs no longer need to exercise their teeth and jaws in order to get enough to eat, they have retained the strong desire to chew and will do so whenever they find something appealing. If owners don't provide their dogs with safe and suitable items to satisfy this urge, they may well find that their dog begins to chew household items, such as shoes and rugs, instead.

What's wrong?

There is little difference between chewing a shoe and chewing the skin of a carcass. Leather is high on the list of a dog's favorite items to chew and needs to be kept out of the way when puppies are growing up. Dogs will develop a preference for the type of material they chewed when young, which, unfortunately, is often leather, plastic, or wood.

ADOLESCENT CHEWING

Owners are often annoyed when their adolescent dog begins to chew enthusiastically, often destroying household items in the process. Being prepared for this stage is just as important as knowing that puppies chew a lot while teething. Adolescent dogs need to chew while their big teeth settle in their jaws and to relieve the frustration of not being able to roam widely to explore their new world. Be sure to provide plenty of suitable things for your dog to chew so that this stage passes without too much frustration or destruction.

This is tasty!

Bones are a natural food source for dogs and most enjoy chewing them. There is a lot of controversy over whether it is safe to let dogs have them, as ingested bones and splinters can cause perforations or compactions in the gut. Despite this danger, many owners allow their dogs to chew on large uncooked bones, and some even offer small soft bones as part of their dog's diet.

It won't hold still.

Puppies need to learn to gnaw on chews provided by their owners rather than household items. Owners should therefore offer a steady stream of different chews as the puppy grows, particularly during teething and during the next phase of intense chewing in adolescence. Dogs that have been bred to use their mouths, such as this Labrador, seem to need to chew more than others.

In the comfort zone

Just like us, our dogs like to relax. This comes as no surprise to their owners, but sometimes they have strange ways of achieving a state of rest, and what they want to do to get comfortable can sometimes be at odds with how their owners would like them to behave. Encouraging dogs to get up on the sofa or bed only teaches them how comfortable it is and, once they have learned to do this, it can be difficult to persuade them to stop.

So comfortable

A dog doesn't learn rules. Once he has learned how pleasant sleeping on the sofa is, he will do so whenever he can. Even if his owner scolds him whenever she catches him, he will feel no guilt in persisting and will simply try to avoid doing so when the owner is close by, to prevent any unpleasantness.

That's better!

Scooting his bottom along the ground helps to relieve any unpleasant feelings or itchiness. Owners can find it embarrassing or distasteful, but dogs such as this one are just trying to get comfortable. This behavior can sometimes indicate that a dog's anal glands are infected or there are other problems in this region, so a veterinary checkup is a good idea.

Just making my bed.

Turning around and around before settling down is a trait inherited from canine ancestors who would need to flatten vegetation to make a comfortable bed. Dogs will do this circling even on carpet where their actions have no effect. This dog pushes at the bedding with her nose as she turns, getting the bedding into just the right place.

Not too hot, not too cold

Trying to maintain a comfortable temperature can produce a range of behaviors that owners find puzzling. Cold dogs may get up on beds or furniture or try to dig a shelter if left outside. Dogs with thick coats like to lie in doorways where the drafts of air cool them down. Dogs cannot produce sweat to cool their skin like humans, and have to rely on panting and other methods to cool down on a hot day.

A refreshing dip

Panting to keep cool requires muscular effort from the ribs to force air over the tongue. This can be exhausting in hot weather and dogs will try to find alternative ways to keep cool. This is especially true for black dogs whose coats absorb the heat from the sun. This dog finds a cooling dip in the sea very pleasant on a hot day.

Just too hot

The hotter the dog, the farther the tongue will protrude in an effort to provide more surface area for evaporation and heat loss. Panting dogs need to drink frequently to replace this fluid or they will not be able to cool themselves down. This dog has been running after a toy and has built up a lot of heat that needs to be expelled.

It's chilly.

Curling up into a ball is a good way to reduce the surface area of the body and, hence, to conserve heat. Dogs usually have a thick undercoat and outer guard hairs providing good insulation. However, due to selective breeding for work and appearance, coats vary hugely and some breeds of dog have more trouble keeping warm than others.

THICK COATS

Some dogs were originally bred to live outside in very cold climates. These dogs will have thick, fluffy undercoats with a strong outer guard-hair layer for insulation. In warmer climates, and especially if kept indoors in centrally heated houses, these dogs often become too hot. They will try anything that keeps them cool and reduces their need for exhausting panting, such as sleeping in drafts, lying down in water dishes, and sticking their heads out of moving car windows.

THE MATING GAME

Winning a mate

Many of the things that dogs do to enable them to breed are instinctive and hardwired into their brains. These include roaming to find mates, an intense interest in other dogs, including scents they have left on the ground, and competition with rivals. These behaviors usually begin at puberty as the body prepares itself for reproduction. For owners, most of these behaviors are tiresome, and many choose to have their dogs neutered or spayed in order to bypass them and to prevent unwanted puppies.

Where is he?

Finding a mate is obviously an essential part of reproduction. Males will escape from home and travel in the direction of a female in season, guided by their scent, which they can detect from many miles away. Females will often try to get out and run off to find a mate on the tenth day of estrus, which is when they are most fertile.

This is my house!

Competition for a place to raise puppies is fierce and at its most intense during estrus when females are ready for mating. Two entire females (ones that have not been spayed) living in a small house together at this time will often fight for the territory, with the stronger dog trying to drive off the other one or even killing her if this behavior cannot be stopped in time.

Get off my patch!

Rivalry between entire males is fierce and there is often competition over territory when two males meet on walks. This rivalry becomes more intense and dogs are more likely to fight if there is a female in estrus close by. Although fights are severe and injuries may be caused before one decides to back down, they are not usually fatal.

Paternal role

If dogs live in a natural pack, the males will have a role providing food for the puppies. In our modern world, male dogs are usually responsible only for passing on their genes. Even if they are not expected to breed, entire male dogs will work hard to find females to mate with, often to the exasperation of their owners. Roaming, searching, mounting, and competitive behaviors are all part of the mating sequence and such instinctive behavior is sometimes impossible to control.

Hold still.

Mounting behavior can be embarrassing for owners but is often enjoyed by entire male dogs. In the absence of a female in estrus, unneutered males will sometimes mount rugs, cuddly toys, people's legs, or small children. Some entire males will never do this, but others do it excessively. There can also be other reasons for this behavior, such as to play or get attention.

Just a minute!

Both male and female puppies will practice mounting behavior during play. Many owners are concerned by this but puppies rarely do it for long. Some puppies that have had limited exposure to other dogs may do it more because it is the only form of play they know. Plenty of socialization with other dogs and puppies will help them learn more acceptable games to play.

Here's my message.

This male West Highland terrier lifts his hind leg as far as he can in order to leave his urine on grass at nose height for other dogs to smell. As well as advertising his presence to potential mates, he is also letting other males know that he is in the area and ready to compete with them if necessary.

Mother love

Maternal behavior is mostly instinctive, although, like all behaviors, improves the more it is practiced. In order to be good mothers, females need to have a good temperament and be comfortable and content in their living conditions. Owners are often amazed at how well their female dogs cope with the production and care of a litter. Good nutrition and plenty of opportunities to socialize and learn about their new world is essential for producing a puppy that will make a good pet for its new family.

You need a cleanup

Very young puppies cannot urinate or defecate unless stimulated to do so. The mother will lick until the puppies relieve themselves, then eat the waste products, keeping the nest clean and free from disease. This behavior is instinctive and does not need to be taught. Keeping a big litter clean and well fed is an exhausting task.

Good to see you again!

Although muzzle licking is no longer necessary to make mothers regurgitate food from a hunt, it continues to be a greeting and bonding mechanism for puppies long after the need to be fed by their mothers has passed. This young puppy is pleased to see her mother returning and licks her face excitedly to show her affection.

Out we go!

As puppies learn to walk, they begin instinctively to move away from the nest to relieve themselves. This keeps the sleeping area clean and reduces risk of disease. Puppies kept in dirty conditions or where there is no difference between nest and play areas may lose this ability to keep clean and will be much harder to house-train.

I'll just go here.

This puppy is sniffing a spot where he has previously been to the toilet. Decaying chemicals in the urine encourage the puppy to want to go on the same spot again. The reassuring presence of the owner ensures that the puppy feels supported, allowing him to relax enough to relieve himself again outside.

INDEX

ACKNOWLEDGMENTS

Executive Editor Trevor Davies
Senior Editor Fiona Robertson
Editor Amy Corbett
Executive Art Editor Sally Bond and Penny Stock
Designer Julie Francis
Production Controller Marian Sumega
Picture Researcher Joanne Forrest Smith

PHOTOGRAPHIC ACKNOWLEDGMENTS

Key: **a** above, **b** below, **c** center, **l** left, **r** right

Alamy Arco Images GmbH 45 al, Blickwinkel 22 br, Isobel Flynn 47 ar, Juniors Bildarchiv 61 al, 63 bl, 75 br, Kathy Hancock 60 c, Nigel Housden 65 a, Peter Titmuss 81 cr, Pictorium 65 bl, tbkmedia.de 9 c. **Animal Photography** R T Willbie 27 al, Sally Anne Thompson 47 bl. **Ardea** Jean Michel Labat 16 c, 33 cl, 58 br, 78 c, John Daniels 59 al, 69 b, 92 c, M Watson 62 cb. **Corbis UK Ltd** Fancy/Veer 15 cl, Radius Images 56 c, Tom Stewart 4 l, 80. **DK Images** Andy Crawford 18 c, Dave King 14 c, David Ward 39 cr, 48 b, Dorling Kindersley 71 b, Emma Firth 44 br, Jane Burton 38 b, 91 ar, Steve Lyne 12 br, 23 bl, 29 ar, Tim Ridley 90 b. **DW Stock Picture Library** Angela Hampton (HR/RM) 79 al. **FLPA** Angela Hampton 41 a, 79 cl, 91 b, Erica Olsen 35 al, 42 br, 86 br, Gerard Lacz 76 br, ImageBroker 21 a, 87 al, ImageBroker/Imagebroker 20 b, 21 cr. **Fotolia** Ant236 55 ar, Callalloo Canis 8 a, 39 al, Cerae 70 br, Claudia Steininger 88 br, Dixi 55 bl, Galina Barskaya 25 al, Geronimo 13 cl, Infinite XX 35 b, Jorge Moro 7 a, Katja Kodba 57 al, Psampaz 83 ar, stoneman 24 c. **Getty Images** Per Breiehagen 61 bl, Tay Jnr 19 br, Todd Pearson 32 c. **Octopus Publishing Group Limited** Russell Sadur 17 al, 77 al, 79 br, 93 bl **Photolibrary** Geoff Higgins 67 bl, Juniors Bildarchiv 40 br, 49 cl, 67 a, 73 ar, Pauline St Denis 75 cl, Ryan McVay 10 br. **Photoshot** NHPA 43 al, NHPA/Susanne Danegger 69 al, NHPA/Yves Laceau 81 a. **RSPCA** Angela Hampton 23 al. **Shutterstock** Cristi Matei 34 cl, Danila 57 bl, Darren Baker 19 al, Galina Barskaya 25 bl, Marina Ljubanovic 45 br, Zelenenkyy Yuriy 89 c. **Superstock** Brand X 84 c, Corbis 23 ar, fStop 61 cr. **The Kennel Club** 25 cr. **Tips Images** Arco Digital Images 17 cr. **Warren Photographic** 1 bc, 2 c, 5 br, 6 b, 11 a & br, 15 a, 17 bl, 26 c, 27 cl, 28 bl, 29 b, 31 ar, 33 ar & r, 34, 36 c, 37 a, 39 bl, 41 cr, 43 b, 46 c, 49 ar & bl, 51 a, bl & cr, 52 b, 53 al & bl, 54 br, 55 c, 59 b, 64 c, 66 b, 72 br, 73 bl, 74 c, 75 a, 77 b, 82, 83 bl, 85 a & cr, 87 cl, 89 a, 93 a & cr. **Your Dog Magazine** 13 ar, 30 cl, 63 a, 71 ar, 31 cl, 37 bl, 50 c, 68 c.